# Poisoned Sunsets

Holly Leemaster

ISBN-13: 978-1723150999

# DEDICATION &
# ACKNOWLEDGEMENTS

I've met so many wonderful souls throughout this life  who have encouraged me to keep going. This book is for you. Most of all, I'd like to thank my mom, my grandpa and grandma Cooley, and my uncle Lanny. Thank you for igniting my creative energy. I'd also like to thank the connections I've made through Instagram, both in person and online. You each bring your own individual flair to my life. I hope that by sharing my vulnerabilities and expressing my story, it will help others to do the same. Finally, this is for anyone who has taken the time to read my words. Especially my best friend; who read the rough draft and kept me sane. That is the greatest gift and I am forever grateful.

Sometimes love is like a match
chucked into a sea
of gasoline:
an intoxication
up in flame.

And when the tide
goes out to play
with hearts of those
left and gone astray,
know that I stand firmly
in my love for you
and only you can
keep my focus.

I write my sins in gold
so at least they'll look
aesthetically pleasing.

# Poisoned Sunsets

Now I'll take what's left
and smear my memories
of you
over pieces left and misused,
hoping to find some solace
in my
broken hearted art.

He liked bleeding hearts
and I guess that's why he
found me.
I liked him more, though,
and that's what drew me in:
the intoxicating need to be near his
  demeanor
and the pull of flowers
that reminded me of sin.

Bleeding from the bone marrow,
your irises explode,
your heart aches with longing
and fear, I suppose.
But you hide behind the pain
and won't let love in
so you left a bleeding heart
to lay here
and let the darkness win.

# Poisoned Sunsets

The sky opened up, broke my heart open
and bled with the pigment
of my unshed tears.
How can something so beautiful
break me even more?

Poisoned sunsets
and the heartbreak glow.
I don't like the person I become
when the sunsets fade
and leave their flow.
I feel erratic,
like I'm grasping at straws.
We fear heartbreak,
but it's already happened.
We fear being abandoned,
but it's already happening.
What we fear most
has already happened.
Nature smirks with knowing shades
and leaves me with
my tempestuous haze.

Holly Leemaster

You're always just out of reach.
Even when you're holding me,
you're still a mile away.
You've never quite
made it close enough to see
that we're both scared
of all the possibilities.

# Poisoned Sunsets

He ripped the wings
from my dreams
and used the blood
to embellish his ego.
The coppery scent
masked the putrid stench
of his insecurity.

Holly Leemaster

Allure and mystery
radiate off your skin.
You pull your baseball cap
down further
and hit me with that
devilish grin.

You turn that baseball cap around
so you can better kiss me.
Your scent intoxicating
until I succumb
to the sound of
my heart beating.

She guards her heart
so wearily;
never letting many people
through the cracks.
Until she's had enough of
her torture –
her heart beats to the fear of
losing control.
You didn't think she'd be a
vixen
in disguise.

I remember what I was wearing
each time you made me feel connected.
Seared like snapshots in my mind.
I hold on to these memories
where I thought you were feeling the same,
but then you got restless
and drifted into another world
without me.
Just like the ocean comes back
to kiss the shore
and recedes into itself once more.

# Poisoned Sunsets

She saw the light in him
that darkness thought it had overthrown.
It teased its way through his fingertips
and played with her hand in his.
He wasn't always cocky,
but it's hard not to understand him
when you share the same hue of rebellion
and you feel the passion in your veins.
She knew what made him tick.
And those who broke him before her
only gave her more of her fix.

Holly Leemaster

So much of what I do
is somehow laced with you;
from my every motion
when I get out of bed
to my dirtiest thought
inked from out of my head.
I don't think I'll ever be done
paying attention to you.

## Poisoned Sunsets

What didn't inspire me
only held me down with gravity
and what didn't consume
my every waking thought
only kept me safe on the balcony.
If an idea or thought or person
doesn't set my soul on fire
I can't get high off the flames
and that's when I'll go searching
for my next desire.

Holly Leemaster

I am more familiar
with endings –
how the sunset ebbs and flows;
how it takes the time to change its mind
and fade slowly for its glow.
Recently, I've found myself
waking for the sun
and the possibilities that you bring
by creating perfection before
the world has begun.

# Poisoned Sunsets

Evocative longing
stretched thin
on a canvas,
lethargically painted
with reminiscence –
slowly, each stoke bringing
the dream to life.
When the fire burns,
you either write it out
or paint its wrath.

If you don't understand her soul,
you miss the whole point of her show.
She breaks to please others;
she'll break every night
just to please the world.
Lighting up the sky
like poisoned sunsets
setting fire to the only
open canvas she's ever known.
She was never meant for superficial,
and there were some that learned too late.
That's why when she breaks for you,
you'll know it was with
everything she could take.

# Poisoned Sunsets

These temporary homes
blocked me from all
the possibilities that roam.

You and poetry
are the only things
worthy of a permanent tattoo.

So I'll take this oath
and the fresh ink from this pen
to write you love letters,
then carve our names
into this tree
that hides my love.

Like a candle slowly
burning out,
you exhaust me
of my oxygen.

# Poisoned Sunsets

You ask me what my
biggest secret is,
so I unpack the masks
of everyone I've ever been.
All lined up in
one big heap,
you choose the one
you want me to keep.
It's got scars and beauty marks,
but you love it just the same.
You say it tells my story
and you want it to remain.

Holly Leemaster

We might have our differences,
but our loneliness is the same.
You were the one to save me
from this terrible disgrace.
Won't you remind me
of us once again?

Like the wild bursts
of a nebula on the
outskirts of oblivion,
you brought color
to my midnight blues.

# Poisoned Sunsets

Afraid of losing control,
the little girl formed
a world of chaos,
wreaking havoc
like a tumultuous flame.

She didn't know what's good for her.
Her brain took its sweet time developing
Worthier decisions.
It's all a dream for her.
Until she caught a glimpse of him.
He was her shot at reality.

You're a fast-paced onlooker,
so concerned with your future,
but I'd rather sit beside you
and take up a residence
with your presence.
Flip through the pages of your past,
keep you grounded
and encourage you
to make these fleeting moments last.

## Poisoned Sunsets

When the world is harsh and critical,
I am thankful for the void.
I am thankful for the people
who don't understand me
so that I could meet the people that do.
I am thankful for my over-caring heart
and overthinking mind
because it adds a flair of peculiarity
that people rarely find.

# Holly Leemaster

I can feel it crackling on the horizon.
That great oblivion before me.
The sense of dread and uncertainty
get tangled in my hair.
I want to be rid of these feelings,
but I sit with them instead.
Welcome     them     with     dreams     and
 infatuations
that linger in my head.

And when this storm resurges,
I'll be there
to welcome
the downpour.

Rebellious angel
with her wings torn off.
No one told her how to fly,
so she wandered off to find a nice guy.
She mistook the devil
for an angel,
and thus,
started her biddings
with the wrong side.

We were never on the same page,
but you made me love
the person I came to be.
And you saw me
for who I wanted to be,
so that's all that ever mattered.
We understood each other's chaos,
but got lost
when it became us.

Months down the road,
I finally understand the phrase
"hindsight is 20/20".
I see it clearly now.
I understand.

## Poisoned Sunsets

You never did know
who's good for your heart;
every bad decision
laced with whiskey.
And you still didn't
know what hit you
when someone enamored
shot you between the eyes.
I guess it's good
I found you and
mirrored your
sweet little lies.

I never wanted the praise;
I wanted the wrath.
Something passionately real
and ours.
Something I could cling to
when the nights got lonely
and the days grew tired.
Someone I could rely on
in the middle of the day
when I can't think of the song.
I know you'll be annoyed to hear me ask,
but your passion for music,
and for me,
will overrule anything.

# Poisoned Sunsets

Let go,
beautiful nightmare,
and find another remedy
for all the pain
that consumes you
when you blackout.
The numb has become an addiction
that you push yourself to the edge
just to recede into the dense fog
once again.

She watched as her life
scattered in front of her –
lyrics to songs
and words chosen carefully;
taken on the wisp of the wind.
It's no longer in her hands.
Her grip slowly let go
of its purpose.

## Poisoned Sunsets

Tell me that I'm poison,
but drink from my soul,
all while ignoring my emptiness.
Tell me that my love is too much
and watch me thrive
in my self-awareness
of madness.

Teach me to question
my self-worth
and stifle my passion
for art.
These are the rules
handed down through the family,
but I'm forcing them to stop
with me.

You moved on and
turned the page,
while I'm left to
drown in your
fading ink.

# Poisoned Sunsets

She was the rain –
all earthy and solaced.
She made you feel like your sadness
wasn't yours to bear alone.
He was the thunder –
loud and all-consuming.
He made you feel
like it's okay to exist.
But when they're together,
they put on quite a show.
Like the way his breath slows
when he falls asleep next to her.
In those moments of striking openness,
she is solely fixed on his presence.
She understood his need to lash out
through her empathetically wild downpours
while she saw glimpses of pain
behind his lightning.
They lent figments of clarity to each other
and together they make
a beautiful thunderstorm.

I like to pretend
that you're hiding your soul
just for my guilty pleasure,
but I've gotten used to
wrapping myself up
in your sins
and coming undone
when you show me
your thoughts within.

## Poisoned Sunsets

I tempt you with my longing gaze
until I see the flames burning in your eyes.
It's all I can do to keep us apart,
but you'll have to entertain these
fantasies.
I'll leave you with
the thought that everything
was real and secrets were never kept.
We both like to tempt fate
and at times it's thrilling
to let our minds wander to
the possibilities of finding out what
we'd be like together.
We're flames in the same raging fire;
souls connected through the trauma.

I've grown familiar with that
muddled wind storm love –
intoxicating, thrilling and over before
the grains had time to settle;
so easily uprooted,
        disheveled,
        forsaken
by any change of current.

I want to know that I'm not
so easily erased,
        eroded,
        eradicated.
I think I'll know when his smile
reaches his laugh lines.

## Poisoned Sunsets

I watched in my peripheral
as you pursed your lips in contemplation.
Lower on my earlobe, you whisper,
trying to decipher me
through sweet nothings.
I rest your hand on my hip
and push it down further.
I don't want to be figured out tonight;
let's just let the moonlight guide us.

The sunset keeps me company
as I ponder life's intricacies.
Are we born good
with the potential to do bad;
or are we born –
needing to be saved.
It's not a question asked often
and it'll make your mind run in circles.
It's intriguing to know
that there are souls out there
who think like me
and don't always wish
for the answers.

## Poisoned Sunsets

I won't settle until your breath
is in my hair
and you curse my name.
I won't succumb to the
complacency of a boring life,
where you never want me
and I'm always out on a binge.
If this life ever comes to that for me,
I'll disappear like the receding fog
and strike places that had always
tempted me,
but were never near enough to taste.

Is it not possible
to be wholly enveloped
in one soul?
Must there always be
competition and silences
made to question relationships.
Will there never be a
certainty other than
I love you more than
you love me.

## Poisoned Sunsets

Unsolicited love:
of all the questions
we should ask
upon meeting someone
of possible interest,
only one truly matters —
do you want my love?

I often wonder
how solitude
heals the heart,
but I've found
it's the greatest healer
after lifetimes
of falling apart.

## Poisoned Sunsets

Time is of the essence,
so make sure it's being shared
with lots of time in nature
and laughter everywhere.
If he doesn't want to invest
in simple things like this,
then send him off with love afar
and let him know he'll be missed.
For it takes a lifetime to figure out
who you want to be;
so why confuse your present being
with questions regarding someone else.

But your soul will live on
long after she forgets
who she wrote
that piece for.
She will write about you
until she exhausts all of her aching soul.
And even then she still might
be able to bleed out some more.
So when she's asked who she wrote
this or that about,
she'll smile with a glimmer of reflection
and a hint of nostalgia.
She'll tell them fondly
it was someone she used to know.

Some people will stand out in the storm
just to feel the rain
and to feel the excitement.
They won't run away.
They will stand out there to meet you
and stay.
Those are the ones
who are worth it.
I would stand
in a thunderstorm
for you.

This was my last ditch effort at healing.
Placing one word in front of the other
instead of smearing mascara down my face.
You see a different side of yourself
when it's two in the morning
and you don't know
what to feel.
Perseverance has never come easily
to a troubled soul like mine,
but it slowly showed its way to me
in these trying times.
I hope it makes its way to you
And offers a little comfort.
I've never been the best
at knowing just what to do,
so please remember my clumsiness
as showing how much I loved you.

# Poisoned Sunsets

Ravenous thoughts crawl
within my mind.
Thoughts of devastation and fear.
A sea of hazy pink wavers for a time
until it all
fades to bleak roving slumber.
I always wanted a dark summer
full of lust and weary eyes,
but I wouldn't be able to give him up
once fall showed up
to my surprise.

I made my way
to your gravestone today
at Beaver Creek Cemetery.
I told you about everything that's happened
since your last day
and how I wish you could see
my brother and me.
You sang those old country songs well
and hummed some military tunes.
I still smell your deodorant
every once in a while
and I catch myself
dreaming of you.
You'll always be with me
just like the songs on the wind
from my favorite cartoon movies.
You didn't know it yet,
but I'll keep you
in my writings
softly tucked behind my pen.

Tell me your stories —

Tell me about your favorite person. Your favorite place. About what you're scared to lose. What you hope to find. Who you want to hurt. About the person that hurt you most. Tell me your stories about what haunts you. What turns you on. Why you can't find the words sometimes. What you love most about yourself. How you see yourself. What keeps you up at night. Who inspires you. Tell me about regret. About want. About life. Tell me where you go to think. Where you want to go. Tell me who you'd be with if society weren't involved. Tell me how you gained confidence. Stories about people you had to let go. Tell me your story and I'll tell you mine.

Holly Leemaster

She's a spitfire with a wild side
and gives her heart to guys
who merely watch
her soul drain from her eyes,
but that doesn't stop her
from giving it all
even when the ones she wants
can't match her unbreakable love
for sunsets and the echoing quiet
of aching country nights.

Poisoned Sunsets

I have many irrational fears:
of people,
of uncertainty,
of instability,
but never
of you.

She rips right through you
like the midwestern wind.
You never know what
hit you
until it's calm once again.

## Poisoned Sunsets

It's funny to me, cowboy,
that you think you have me figured out.
I wonder what's keeping you stumped
on that high horse you ride around.

You set your sights on me,
but, darling,
I'm a moving target.

You're more than what your mind says
when you don't conform to society.

Let the loneliness consume you
if only for a night.

When you're annoyed with someone else
take the time to look within.
I know it doesn't seem like it,
but your mind needs your attention.
It wants to bring you back to yourself
when you are all you have.
Stay with these feelings
and welcome them at the door,
but all the while,
keep searching for more.

## Poisoned Sunsets

Your grin shows up
like a pistol quickly drawn.
I have no time for the
instant shock.
You pull the trigger
and I'm gone.

Silence proceeds her chaotic strikes.
That's what the storm clouds say.
They whisper and crackle with her talent,
slowly rolling in on the breeze.

The rain never bothered me.
It was always the charge
in the atmosphere
that I had to worry about.
I was too tempted to run away
with the storm.

# ABOUT THE AUTHOR

Holly Leemaster loves online quizzes, psychology, walking her dog through the woods, and spending time with her mom and brother on the farm. If she has free time on the weekend, she can be found at bookstores, county fairs in the summer, watching movies with her friends, or perusing social media for writing ideas. She's worked at her local library for almost six years and recently attained a bachelor's degree in liberal studies from Bowling Green State University.

Instagram: @musingsbyholly

Made in the USA
Middletown, DE
07 September 2018